Malcolm X

Black Muslim Leader

Filiquarian Publishing, LLC.

Malcolm X

Black Muslim Leader

Malcolm X (born Malcolm Little; May 19, 1925 – February 21, 1965), also known as El-Hajj Malik El-Shabazz,[1] was an American Black Muslim minister and a spokesman for the Nation of Islam.

After leaving the Nation of Islam in 1964, he made the pilgrimage, the Hajj, to Mecca and became a Sunni Muslim. He also founded the Muslim Mosque, Inc. and the Organization of Afro-American Unity. Less than a year later, he was assassinated in Washington Heights on the first day of National Brotherhood Week.

Historian Robin D.G. Kelley wrote, "Malcolm X has been called many things: Pan-Africanist, father of Black Power, religious fanatic, closet conservative, incipient socialist, and a menace to society. The meaning of his public life — his politics and ideology — is contested in part because his entire body of work consists of a few dozen speeches and a collaborative autobiography whose veracity is challenged.... Malcolm has become a sort of tabula rasa, or blank slate, on which people of different positions can write their own interpretations of his politics and legacy. Chuck D of the rap group Public Enemy and Supreme Court Justice Clarence Thomas can both declare Malcolm X their hero."[2]

Early Years

Malcolm Little was born in 1925 in Omaha, Nebraska, to Earl Little and Louise Helen (née Norton). He lived briefly at 3448 Pinkney Street in the North Omaha neighborhood. His father was an outspoken Baptist lay speaker and supporter of Marcus Garvey, as well as a member of the Universal Negro Improvement Association.[3] Three of Earl Little's brothers died violently at the hands of white men, and one of his uncles had been lynched.[4]

Earl Little had three children (Ella, Mary, and Earl, Jr.) by a previous marriage before he married Malcolm's mother. From his second marriage he had eight children, of whom Malcolm was the fourth. Earl and Louise Little's children's names were, in order, Wilfred, Hilda, Philbert, Malcolm, Reginald, Wesley, Yvonne, and Robert.

Louise Little was born in Grenada, and Malcolm said she looked like a white woman. Her father was a white man of whom Malcolm knew nothing except what he described as his mother's shame. Malcolm got his light complexion from him. Initially he felt it was a status symbol to be light-skinned, but later he would say that he "hated every drop of that white rapist's blood that is in me." As Malcolm was the lightest child in the family, he felt that his father favored him; however, his mother treated him harshly for the same reason.[5] One of his nicknames, "Red," derived from the reddish tinge of his hair. He was described as having, at birth, "ash-blonde hair ... tinged with cinnamon," and at four, "reddish-blonde hair." His hair darkened as he aged but also resembled the hair of his paternal grandmother, whose hair "turned reddish in the summer sun."[6]

According to The Autobiography of Malcolm X, his mother had been threatened by Ku Klux Klansmen while she was pregnant with him in December 1924. His mother recalled the Klansmen warned the family to leave Omaha, because Earl Little's activities with UNIA were "stirring up trouble".[7]

The family relocated to Milwaukee, Wisconsin, in 1926, and to Lansing, Michigan, shortly after. In 1931, Malcolm's father was found dead, having been run over by a streetcar in Lansing. Authorities ruled his death a suicide.[8] Malcolm said that the black community disputed the cause of death. His family had frequently found themselves the target of harassment by the Black Legion, a white supremacist group his father accused of burning down their home in 1929, and many blacks felt that the Black Legion had killed Earl Little.[9] Malcolm doubted that his father could "bash himself in the head, then get down across the streetcar tracks to be run over."[10]

Though Malcolm's father had two life insurance policies, his mother received death benefits solely from the smaller policy. Malcolm said the insurance company that had issued the larger policy accepted the police determination that Earl Little's death had been a suicide, and accordingly refused to pay.[10] Louise Little had a nervous breakdown and was declared legally insane in December 1938. Malcolm and his siblings were split up and sent to different foster homes. Louise Little was formally committed to the state mental hospital at Kalamazoo, Michigan. She remained there until Malcolm and his brothers and sisters secured her release 26 years later.

In his Autobiography, written more than 25 years later, Malcolm said that after the death of his father he lived on Charles Street in downtown East Lansing. The 1930 U.S. Census showed him living on a different Charles Street, in the low-income Urbandale neighborhood in Lansing Township, between Lansing and East Lansing. Later, when he was in high school, Malcolm Little lived in Mason, an almost all-white small town 12 miles (19 km) to the south.

Malcolm Little graduated from junior high school at the top of his class but dropped out soon after a teacher told him that his aspirations of being a lawyer were "no realistic goal for a nigger".[11] After enduring a series of foster homes, Malcolm was sent to a detention center. Then he moved to Boston to live with his older half-sister, Ella Little Collins. In Boston he held a variety of jobs and intermittently found employment with the New Haven Railroad. In 1942, at age 17, Malcolm became "involved with Boston's underworld fringe."[7]

Young Adult Years

Malcolm left Boston to live for a short time in Detroit and Inkster, Michigan. He moved to New York City in 1943. There he worked again briefly for the New Haven Railroad. Malcolm found work as a shoeshiner at a Lindy Hop nightclub. In The Autobiography of Malcolm X, he said that he once shined the shoes of Duke Ellington and other notable African-American musicians. After some time in Harlem, he became involved in drug dealing, gambling, racketeering, robbery and steering prostitutes. During this time, his friends and acquaintances called him "Detroit Red".[12] Between 1943 and 1946, when he was arrested and jailed in Massachusetts, Malcolm drifted between Boston and New York City three more times.[7]

When Malcolm was examined for the draft, military physicians classified him to be "mentally disqualified for military service." He explained in his autobiography that he put on a display to avoid the draft by telling the examining officer that he could not wait to "kill some crackers." His approach worked. His classification ensured he would not be drafted.[13]

In early 1946, Malcolm returned to Boston. On January 12, he was arrested for burglary trying to steal a stolen watch he had left for repairs at a jewelry shop. Two days later, Malcolm was indicted for carrying firearms. On January 16, he was charged with Grand Larceny and Breaking and Entering. Malcolm was sentenced to eight to ten years in Massachusetts State Prison.[7]

On February 27, Malcolm began serving his sentence at the Massachusetts State Prison in Charlestown. While in prison, Malcolm earned the nickname of "Satan" for his vitriolic hatred towards the Bible, God and religion in general.[14] Malcolm began reading books from the prison library. Soon he developed a voracious appetite for reading, then astigmatism. His brother Reginald wrote letters describing his experience with the Nation of Islam, and Malcolm decided to convert.

For the remainder of his incarceration, Malcolm maintained regular contact with Elijah Muhammad, the group's leader. Malcolm started to gain fame among the prisoners but also remained under the eye of the authorities. He was denied a possible early release after five years.

In February 1948, mostly through his sister's efforts, Malcolm was transferred to an experimental prison in Norfolk, Massachusetts, a facility that had a much larger library. Malcolm later reflected on his time in prison: "Months passed without my even thinking about being imprisoned. In fact, up to then, I had never been so truly free in my life."[14] On August 7, 1952, Malcolm received parole and was released from prison.[7]

Nation of Islam

In 1952, after his release from prison, Malcolm went to meet Elijah Muhammad in Chicago. Soon after their meeting, he changed his surname to "X". Malcolm explained the name by saying, "The 'X' is meant to symbolize the rejection of 'slave names' and the absence of an inherited African name to take its place. The 'X' is also the brand that many slaves received on their upper arm." This was the rationale that led many members of the Nation of Islam to change their surnames to X.

In March 1953, the FBI opened a file on Malcolm X, after hearing that he had described himself as a Communist. Included in the file were two letters wherein Malcolm used the alias "Malachi Shabazz". In Message to the Blackman in America, Elijah Muhammad explained the name Shabazz as belonging to descendants of an "Asian Black nation".

In May 1953, the FBI concluded that Malcolm had an "asocial personality with paranoid trends (pre-psychotic paranoid schizophrenia)", and had, in fact, sought treatment for his disorder. This was further supported by a letter intercepted by the FBI, dated June 29, 1950. The letter said, in reference to his 4-F classification and rejection by the military, "Everyone has always said ... Malcolm is crazy, so it isn't hard to convince people that I am."[15]

Later that year, Malcolm left his half-sister Ella in Boston to stay with Elijah Muhammad in Chicago. He soon returned to Boston and became the minister of the Nation of Islam's Temple Number Eleven.

In 1954, Malcolm was selected to lead the Nation of Islam's Temple Number Seven on Lenox Avenue in Harlem. He rapidly expanded its membership. After a local television broadcast in New York City about the Nation of Islam, Malcolm became known to a wider audience. Representatives of the print media, radio, and television frequently asked Malcolm for comments on issues. He was also sought as a spokesman by reporters from other countries.

From his adoption of the Nation of Islam in 1952 until he left the organization in 1964, Malcolm X promoted the Nation's teachings. He referred to whites as "devils" who had been created in a misguided breeding program by lack scientist, and predicted the inevitable (and imminent) return of blacks to their natural place at the top of the social order.

Malcolm was considered the second most influential leader of the movement, after Elijah Muhammad. He opened additional temples, including one in Philadelphia. He was largely credited with increasing membership in the Nation of Islam from 500 in 1952 to 30,000 in 1963. He inspired the boxer Cassius Clay (later known as Muhammad Ali) to join the Nation of Islam. (Like Malcolm, Ali later left the Nation of Islam and joined mainstream Islam.)

Marriage and Family

In 1958, Malcolm married Betty X (née Sanders) in Lansing, Michigan. They had six daughters, all of whom carried the family name of Shabazz. Their names were Attallah, born in 1958; Qubilah, born in 1960; Ilyasah, born in 1962; Gamilah (also spelled Gumilah), born in 1964; and twins,

Malaak and Malikah, born after Malcolm's death in 1965.

Meeting Castro

In September 1960, Malcolm met with Fidel Castro during Castro's visit to the United Nations in New York. Malcolm was a prominent member of a Harlem-based welcoming committee made up of black community leaders that greeted heads of state, particularly those from African countries, who had come to New York to address the UN General Assembly.

Tensions and Departure from the Nation of Islam

In early 1963, Malcolm started collaborating with Alex Haley on The Autobiography of Malcolm X. The book had not been finalized at the time of Malcolm's assassination in 1965. Haley completed it and published it later that year.[16]

Writing after his break from the Nation of Islam, Malcolm said in the Autobiography that one reason for the separation was growing tension between him and Elijah Muhammad that arose from Malcolm's dismay at rumors of Muhammad's extramarital affairs with young secretaries. These rumors troubled Malcolm because the Nation of Islam condemns adultery. At first Malcolm brushed these rumors aside. Later, he spoke with Elijah Muhammad's son and the women making the accusations and he came to believe them. According to the Autobiography, in 1963 Elijah Muhammad confirmed the rumors to Malcolm. Muhammad justified his actions by saying they followed a pattern established by Biblical prophets.

Malcolm criticized the 1963 March on Washington, which he called "the farce on Washington". He said he didn't know why black people were excited over a demonstration "run by whites in front of a statue of a president who has been dead for a hundred years and who didn't like us when he was alive."

When asked for a comment about the assassination of President Kennedy in November 1963, Malcolm said that it was a case of "the chickens coming home to roost." He added that

"Chickens coming home to roost never made me sad. It only made me glad." This remark prompted a widespread public outcry. The Nation of Islam publicly censured their former shining star. Although Malcolm retained his post and rank as minister, Elijah Muhammad banned him from public speaking for 90 days.

Malcolm publicly announced his break from the Nation of Islam on March 8, 1964. He founded the Muslim Mosque, Inc. four days later. Malcolm stayed close to some of the teachings of the Nation of Islam but began modifying them. He explicitly advocated political and economic black nationalism, as opposed to the Nation of Islam's religious nationalism. In April, he made a speech titled "The Ballot or the Bullet." Malcolm was in contact with several orthodox Muslims, who encouraged him to learn about orthodox Islam. He soon converted to orthodox Islam, and decided to make his pilgrimage to Mecca.

Pilgrimage to Mecca

On April 13, 1964, Malcolm departed JFK Airport, New York for Cairo by way of Frankfurt.

It was the second time Malcolm had been to Africa. On the next leg of his journey, Malcolm left Cairo for Jeddah, Saudi Arabia. His status as an authentic Muslim was questioned by Saudi authorities because of his inability to speak Arabic and his United States passport. Since only confessing Muslims are allowed into Mecca, he was separated from the group with which he arrived and was isolated. He spent about 20 hours wearing the ihram, a two-piece garment comprising two white unhemmed sheets.

According to the Autobiography, Malcolm X remembered the book The Eternal Message of Muhammad by Abdul Rahman Hassan Azzam, which Dr. Mahmoud Yousseff Sharwabi had presented with his visa approval. He called Azzam's son, who arranged for his release. At the younger Azzam's home, he met Azzam Pasha, who gave Malcolm his suite at the Jeddah Palace Hotel. The next morning, Muhammad Faisal, the son of Prince Faisal, visited and informed Malcolm X that he was to be a state guest. The deputy chief of protocol accompanied Malcolm X to the Hajj Court, where he was allowed to make his pilgrimage.

On April 19, Malcolm completed the Umrah, making the seven circuits around the Kaaba, drinking from the Zamzam Well and running between the hills of Safah and Marwah seven times. According to the Autobiography, on this trip Malcolm viewed Muslims of different races interacting as equals and came to believe that Islam could transcend racial problems.

International Travel

Africa

Malcolm X visited Africa on three separate occasions, once in 1959 and twice in 1964. During his visits, he met officials, as well as spoke on television and radio in: Cairo, Egypt; Addis Ababa, Ethiopia; Dar Es Salaam, Tanganyika (now Tanzania); Lagos and Ibadan, Nigeria; Accra, Winneba, and Legon, Ghana; Conakry, Guinea; Algiers, Algeria; and Casablanca, Morocco.

Malcolm first went to Africa in summer of 1959. He traveled to Egypt (United Arab Republic),

Sudan, Nigeria and Ghana to arrange a tour for
Elijah Muhammad, which occurred in December
1959. The first of Malcolm's two trips to Africa in
1964 lasted from April 13 until May21. On May 8,
following his speech at Trenchard Hall on the
campus of the University of Ibadan in Nigeria, he
attended a reception in the Students' Union Hall
held for him by the Muslim Students' Society.
During this reception the students bestowed upon
him the name "Omowale", meaning "the son
returns home" in the Yoruba language.

Malcolm returned to New York from Africa via
Paris on May 21, 1964. On July 9, he again left the
U.S. for Africa, spending a total of 18 weeks
abroad. On July 17, 1964, Malcolm addressed the
Organization of African Unity's first ordinary
assembly of heads of state and governments in
Cairo as a representative of the OAAU. On
August 21, 1964, he made a press statement on
behalf of the OAAU regarding the second African
summit conference of the OAU. In it, he explained
how a strong and independent "United States of
Africa" is a victory for the awakening of African
Americans. By the time he returned to the United
States on November 24, 1964, Malcolm had

established an international connection between Africans on the continent and those in the diaspora.

Malcolm held to the view that African-Americans were right in defending themselves from aggressors. On June 28, 1964, at the founding rally of the OAAU he said,

"The time for you and me to allow ourselves to be brutalized nonviolently has passed. Be nonviolent only with those who are nonviolent to you. And when you can bring me a nonviolent racist, bring me a nonviolent segregationist, then I'll get nonviolent. But don't teach me to be nonviolent until you teach some of those crackers to be nonviolent."[17]

In an interview with Gordon Parks in 1965, Malcolm revealed:

"I realized racism isn't just lack and white problem. It's brought bloodbaths to about every nation on earth at one time or another. Brother, remember the time that white college girl came into the restaurant — the one who wanted to help

the [Black] Muslims and the whites get together
— and I told her there wasn't a ghost of a chance
and she went away crying? Well, I've lived to
regret that incident. In many parts of the African
continent I saw white students helping black
people. Something like this kills a lot of argument.
I did many things as a [Black] Muslim that I'm
sorry for now. I was a zombie then — like all
[Black] Muslims — I was hypnotized, pointed in a
certain direction and told to march. Well, I guess a
man's entitled to make a fool of himself if he's
ready to pay the cost. It cost me 12 years. That
was ad scene, brother. The sickness and madness
of those days — I'm glad to be free of them."

France and the UK

In late 1964, Malcolm visited France together with
Jamaican officials and spoke in Paris at Salle
Pleyel where there were discussions and debates
on the subject of the Rastafarian ideas espoused by
both the Jamaicans present and Malcolm X at that
time. He also visited the UK and participated in a
debate at the Oxford Union on December 3,
1964.[18]

On February 12, 1965, Malcolm visited Smethwick, near Birmingham, which had become a byword for racial division after the 1964 general election when the Conservative Party won the parliamentary seat using the slogan, among others, "If you want a nigger for your neighbour, vote Labour".[19] He visited a pub with a "non-coloured" policy and visited a street where the local council would buy houses and sell them to white families, to avoid black families moving in.

Death and Afterwards

Assassination

Tensions increased between Malcolm and the Nation of Islam. It was alleged that orders were given by leaders of the Nation of Islam to "destroy" Malcolm; in The Autobiography of Malcolm X, he says that as early as 1963, a member of the Seventh Temple confessed to him having received orders from the Nation of Islam to kill him.

On March 20, 1964, Life published a photograph of Malcolm holding an M1 Carbine and pulling back the curtains to peer out of the window of his family's home. The photo was taken in connection with Malcolm's declaration that he would defend himself from the daily death threats which he and his family were receiving. Undercover FBI informants warned officials that he had been marked for assassination.

In June 1964, the NOI sued to reclaim Malcolm's home in Queens, which they claimed belonged to the organization. The suit was successful, and Malcolm and his family were ordered to vacate the house. On February 14, 1965, the night before a scheduled hearing to postpone the eviction date, the house burned to the ground. Malcolm and his family survived, and no one was charged with any crime.

On February 21, 1965 in Manhattan's Audubon Ballroom, Malcolm had just begun delivering a speech when a disturbance broke out in the crowd of 400. A man yelled, "Get your hand outta my pocket! Don't be messin' with my pockets!" As Malcolm and his bodyguards moved to quiet the disturbance,[20] a man rushed forward and shot Malcolm in the chest with a sawed-off shotgun.

Two other men charged the stage and fired handguns at Malcolm, who was shot 16 times. Angry onlookers in the crowd caught and beat the assassins as they attempted to flee the ballroom. Malcolm was pronounced dead on arrival at New York's Columbia Presbyterian Hospital.

Two suspects were named by witnesses — Norman 3X Butler and Thomas 15X Johnson, both members of the Nation of Islam.

Three men were eventually charged in the case. Talmadge Hayer, also a Black Muslim, confessed to having fired shots into Malcolm's body, but he testified that Butler and Johnson were not present and were not involved in the shooting. All three were convicted.

Funeral

Malcolm's body was made available for public viewing in Harlem's Unity Funeral Home from February 23 through February 26, 1965, and the number of mourners who filed past his body has been estimated between 14,000 and 30,000.[21] Malcolm's funeral was held on February 27, 1965, at the Faith Temple Church of God in Christ, also in Harlem. The Church was filled to capacity, with more than 1,700 people. Ossie Davis delivered a eulogy, describing Malcolm as "our shining black prince."

"There are those who will consider it their duty, as friends of the Negro people, to tell us to revile him, to flee, even from the presence of his memory, to save ourselves by writing him out of the history of our turbulent times. Many will ask what Harlem finds to honor in this stormy, controversial and bold young captain — and we will smile. Many will say turn away — away from this man, for he is not a man but a demon, a monster, a subverter and an enemy of the black man — and we will smile. They will say that he is of hate — a fanatic, a racist — who can only bring evil to the cause for which you struggle! And we will answer and say to them: Did you ever talk to Brother Malcolm? Did you ever touch him, or have him smile at you? Did you ever really listen to him? Did he ever do a mean thing? Was he ever himself associated with violence or any public disturbance? For if you did you would know him.

And if you knew him you would know why we must honor him."[22]

Malcolm X was buried at the Ferncliff Cemetery in Hartsdale, New York. At the gravesite after the ceremony, friends took the shovels away from the waiting gravediggers and buried Malcolm themselves. Later that month, actors Ruby Dee and Sidney Poitier became co-chairs of the New York affiliate of the Educational Fund for the Children of Malcolm X Shabazz.

Response to Malcolm's Death

After Malcolm's death, Martin Luther King, Jr., sent a telegram to Betty Shabazz, expressing his sadness over "the shocking and tragic assassination of your husband."

"While we did not always see eye to eye on methods to solve the race problem, I always had a deep affection for Malcolm and felt that he had a great ability to put his finger on the existence and the root of the problem. He was an eloquent spokesman for his point of view and no one can honestly doubt that Malcolm had a great concern for the problems we face as a race."[23]

Elijah Muhammad reacted differently; as he told the annual Savior's Day convention on February 26, "Malcolm X got just what he preached."[24]

The international press, particularly that of Africa, was sympathetic. The Daily Times of Nigeria wrote,

"Like all mortals, Malcolm X was not without his faults ... but that he was a dedicated and consistent disciple of the movement for the emancipation of his brethren no one can doubt. ... Malcolm X has fought and died for what he believed to be right. He will have a place in the palace of martyrs."[25]

Kwangming, published in Beijing, bluntly stated that "Malcolm was murdered because he fought for freedom and equal rights."[26]

Conspiracy Theories

Within days of Malcolm's assassination, questions were raised about who was responsible for his death. On February 23, James Farmer, the leader of the Congress of Racial Equality, announced at a news conference that local drug dealers, and not the Black Muslims, were to blame.[27] Others blamed the police, the FBI, or the CIA, citing the lack of police protection and the ease with which the assassins had entered the Audubon Ballroom.[28]

In the 1970s, the public learned about COINTELPRO and other secret government programs to infiltrate and disrupt civil rights organizations during the 1950s and 1960s. John Ali, national secretary of the Nation of Islam, has been identified as an FBI agent.[29] Malcolm had confided in a reporter that Ali had exacerbated tensions between him and Elijah Muhammad, and he considered Ali his "archenemy" within the Nation of Islam leadership.[29] On February 20, the night before the assassination, Ali met with Hayer, one of the men convicted of killing Malcolm.[30]

Popular Culture

The film Malcolm X was released in 1992, directed by Spike Lee and based on the autobiography. It starred Denzel Washington as Malcolm, with Angela Bassett as Betty and Al Freeman, Jr. as Elijah Muhammad. Both Roger Ebert and Martin Scorsese named the film as one of the 10 best of the decade.

The 2001 film Ali also features Malcolm X, as played by Mario Van Peebles.

Black Muslim Leader

References

1. This name includes the honorific El-Hajj, which he was entitled to use as a Muslim who had completed the Hajj to Mecca.

2. Robin D.G. Kelley, "Malcolm X", Africana: The Encyclopedia of the African and African American Experience (New York: Basic Civitas Books, 1999), ISBN 0-465-00071-1.

3. David Haward Bain, The Old Iron Road: An Epic of Rails, Roads, and the Urge to Go West (Penguin Books, 2004, ISBN 0-14-303526-6), pp. 65-66.

4. The Autobiography of Malcolm X, p. 2.

5. The Autobiography of Malcolm X, pp. 2-3.

6. Bruce Perry, Malcolm: The Life of a Man Who Changed Black America (Station Hill Press, 1991, ISBN 0-88268-103-6), pp. 2, 4.

7. Chronology of the Life and Activities of Malcolm X, Malcolm X: A Research Site.

8. Assassination of Malcolm X, Black Muslim, The Crime Library.

9. Malcolm X 1925-1965, Muslim American Society.

10. The Autobiography of Malcolm X, p. 11.

11. The Autobiography of Malcolm X, p. 36.

12. Transcript, Malcolm X: Make It Plain, American Experience, PBS.

13. Ferruccio Gambino, The Transgression of a Laborer: Malcom X in the Wilderness of America, Radical History, Winter 1993.

14. Mass Moments: Malcolm X Imprisoned, February 27, 1946.

15. FBI report, Malcolm K. Little [sic], May 4, 1953, p.3. Available online, p. 7.

16. In 1964, Malcolm told Haley, "If I'm alive when this book comes out, it will be a miracle." Alex Haley, Epilogue, The Autobiography of Malcolm X, p. 410.

17. Malcolm X, OAAU Founding Rally.

18. Malcolm X Oxford Debate, Malcolm X: A Research Site.

19. National Extension College, A2 Government & Politics, Topic 4 – Race and ethnicity, p. 4.

20. In the Epilogue to The Autobiography of Malcolm X, Alex Haley wrote that Malcolm said, "Hold it! Hold it! Don't get excited. Let's cool it brothers." (p. 434.) According to a transcription of a recording of the shooting, Malcolm's only words were, "Hold it!", which he repeated 10 times. (Louis A. DeCaro, Jr., On the Side of My People: A Religious Life of Malcolm X (New York University Press, 1996, ISBN 0-8147-1864-7), p. 274.)

21. Perry, p. 374. Alex Haley, in his Epilogue to The Autobiography of Malcolm X, says 22,000 (p. 452).

22. Ossie Davis, Eulogy delivered at the funeral of Malcolm X, Faith Temple Church Of God, February 27, 1965.

23. Martin Luther King, Jr., Telegram to Betty Shabazz, February 26, 1965.

24. Karl Evanzz, The Judas Factor: The Plot to Kill Malcolm X (Thunder's Mouth Press, 1992, ISBN 1-56025-049-6) p. 301.

25. Evanzz, p. 305.

26. Evanzz, p. 306.

27. Perry, p. 371.

28. Perry, p. 372.

29. Louis E. Lomax, To Kill a Black Man, (Holloway House, 1968, ISBN 0-87067-731-4), p. 198.

30. Evanzz, p. 294.

Black Muslim Leader

Further Reading

By Malcolm X

* The Autobiography of Malcolm X. With the assistance of Alex Haley. New York: Grove Press, 1965.

* By Any Means Necessary: Speeches, Interviews, and a Letter by Malcolm X. George Breitman, ed. New York: Pathfinder, 1970.

* The End of White World Supremacy: Four Speeches by Malcolm X. Benjamin Karim, ed. New York: Seaver Books, 1971.

* Malcolm X: February 1965, The Final Speeches. Steve Clark, ed. New York: Pathfinder, 1992.

* Malcolm X: The Last Speeches. Bruce Perry, ed. New York: Pathfinder, 1989.

* Malcolm X Speaks Out (A Callaway BoundSound Book with Compact Disc). Nan Richardson, Catherine Chermayeff, and Antoinette

White, eds. Kansas City, MO: Andrews and McMeel, 1992.

* Malcolm X Speaks: Selected Speeches and Statements. George Breitman, ed. New York: Merit Publishers, 1965.

* Notes from the Frontlines: Excerpts from the Great Speeches of Malcolm X (Compact Disc). BMG Music, 1992.

* The Speeches of Malcolm X at Harvard. Archie Epps, ed. New York: Morrow, 1968.

* The Wisdom of Malcolm X (Compact Discs). Black Label, 1991.

Articles

* Parks, Gordon. The White Devil's Day is Almost Over. Life, May 31, 1963.

* Speakman, Lynn. Who Killed Malcolm X? The Valley Advocate, November 26, 1992, pp. 3-6.

* Vincent, Theodore. The Garveyite Parents of Malcolm X. The Black Scholar, vol. 20, #2, April, 1989.

* Handler ,M.S.Malcolm X cites role in U.N. Fight. New York Times, Jan 2, 1965; pg. 6,1.

* Montgomery, Paul L. Malcolm X a Harlem Idol on Eve of Murder Trial. New York Times, Dec 6, 1965; pg. 46, 1

* Bigart, Homer. Malcolm X-ism Feared by Rustin. New York Times, Mar 4, 1965; pg. 15, 1

* Arnold, Martin. Harlem is Quiet as Crowds Watch Malcolm X Rites. New York Times, Feb 28, 1965; pg. 1, 2

* Loomis, James. Death of Malcolm X. New York Times. Feb 27, 1965; pg. 24, 1

* n/a. Malcolm X and Muslims. New York Times, Feb 21, 1965; pg. E10, 1

* n/a. Malcolm X. New York Times, Feb 22, 1965; pg. 20, 1

* n/a. Malcolm X Reports He Now Represents Muslim World Unit. New York Times, Oct 11, 1964; pg. 13, 1

* Lelyveld, Joseph. Elijah Muhammad Rallies His Followers in Harlem. New York Times, Jun 29, 1964; pg. 1, 2

* n/a. Malcolm X Woos 2 Rights Leaders. New York Times, May 19, 1964; pg. 28, 1

* n/a. 1,000 In Harlem Cheer Malcolm X. New York Times, Mar 23, 1964; pg. 18, 1

* Handler, M.S. Malcolm X Sees Rise in Violence. New York Times, Mar 13, 1964; pg. 20, 1

* n/a. Malcolm X Disputes Nonviolence Policy. New York Times, Jun 5, 1963; pg. 29, 1

* Apple, R.W. Malcolm X Silenced for Remarks On Assassination of Kennedy. New York Times, Dec 5, 1963; pg. 22, 1

* Ronan, Thomas P. Malcolm X Tells Rally In Harlem Kennedy Fails to Help Negroes. New York Times, Jun 30, 1963; pg. 45, 1

* n/a. 4 Are Indicted Here in Malcolm X Case. New York Times, Mar 11, 1965; pg. 66, 1

* Handler, M.S. Malcolm X Seeks U.N. Negro Debate. Special to The New York Times; New York Times, Aug 13, 1964; pg. 22, 1

Books

* Acuna, Rodolfo. Occupied America: A History of Chicanos. New York: Harper & Row, 1981.

* Alkalimat, Abdul. Malcolm X for Beginners. New York: Writers and Readers, 1990.

* Als, Hilton. "The Women." (a chapter on Malcolm's mother)

* Asante, Molefi K. Malcolm X as Cultural Hero: and Other Afrocentric Essays. Trenton, N.J.: Africa World Press, 1993.

* Baldwin, James. One Day, When I Was Lost: A Scenario Based On Alex Haley's "The Autobiography Of Malcolm X". New York: Dell, 1992.

* Breitman, George. The Last Year of Malcolm X: The Evolution of a Revolutionary. New York: Pathfinder, 1967.

* Breitman, George, and Herman Porter. The Assassination of Malcolm X. New York: Pathfinder, 1976.

* Brisbane, Robert. Black Activism. Valley Forge, Pennsylvania: Judson Press, 1974.

* Carew, Jan. Ghosts In Our Blood: With Malcolm X in Africa, England, and the Caribbean. Chicago: Lawrence Hill, 1994.

* Carson, Claybourne. Malcolm X: The FBI File. New York: Carroll & Graf, 1991.

* Carson, Claybourne, et al. The Eyes on the Prize Civil Rights Reader. New York: Penguin, 1991.

* Clarke, John Henrik, ed. Malcolm X; the Man and His Times. New York: Macmillan, 1969.

* Cleage, Albert B., and George Breitman. Myths About Malcolm X: Two Views. New York: Merit, 1968.

* Collins, Rodney P. The Seventh Child. New York: Dafina; London: Turnaround, 2002.

* Cone, James H. Martin & Malcolm & America: A Dream or A Nightmare. Maryknoll, N.Y.: Orbis Books, 1991.

* Davis, Thulani. Malcolm X: The Great Photographs. New York: Stewart, Tabon and Chang, 1992.

* DeCaro, Louis A. Malcolm and the Cross: The Nation of Islam, Malcolm X, and Christianity. New York: New York University, 1998.

* DeCaro, Louis A. On The Side of My People: A Religious Life of Malcolm X. New York: New York University, 1996.

* Doctor, Bernard Aquina. Malcolm X for Beginners. New York: Writers and Readers, 1992.

* Dyson, Michael Eric. Making Malcolm: The Myth and Meaning of Malcolm X. New York: Oxford University Press, 1996.

* Essien-Udom, E. U. Black Nationalism. Chicago: University of Chicago Press, 1962.

* Evanzz, Karl. The Judas Factor: The Plot to Kill Malcolm X. New York: Thunder's Mouth Press, 1992.

* Franklin, Robert Michael. Liberating Visions: Human Fulfillment And Social Justice In African-American Thought. Minneapolis, MN : Fortress Press, 1990.

* Friedly, Michael. The Assassination of Malcolm X. New York: Carroll & Graf, 1992.

* Gallen, David, ed. Malcolm A to Z: The Man and His Ideas. New York: Carroll and Graf, 1992.

* Gallen, David, ed. Malcolm X: As They Knew Him. New York: Carroll and Graf, 1992.

* Garrow, David. Bearing the Cross: Martin Luther King, Jr. and the Southern Christian Leadership Conference. New York: Vintage, 1988.

* Goldman, Peter. The Death and Life of Malcolm X. Urbana: University of Illinois Press, 1979.

* Hampton, Henry, and Steve Fayer. Voices of Freedom: Oral Histories from the Civil Rights Movement from the 1950s Through the 1980s. New York: Bantam, 1990.

* Harding, Vincent, Robin D. G. Kelley, and Earl Lewis. We Changed the World: African Americans, 1945-1970. The Young Oxford History of African Americans, v.9. New York: Oxford University Press, 1997.

* Hill, Robert A. Marcus Garvey: Life and Lessons. Los Angeles: University of California Press, 1987.

* Jamal, Hakim A. From The Dead Level: Malcolm X and Me. New York: Random House, 1972.

* Jenkins, Robert L. The Malcolm X Encyclopedia. Westport, Conn.: Greenwood Press, 2002.

* Karim, Benjamin, with Peter Skutches and David Gallen. Remembering Malcolm. New York: Carroll & Graf, 1992.

* Kly, Yussuf Naim, ed. The Black Book: The True Political Philosophy of Malcolm X (El Hajj Malik El Shabazz). Atlanta: Clarity Press, 1986.

* Kondo, Baba Zak A. Conspiracys: Unravelling the Assassination of Malcolm X. Washington, D.C.: Nubia Press, 1993.

* Leader, Edward Roland. Understanding Malcolm X: The Controversial Changes in His Political Philosophy. New York: Vantage Press, 1993.

* Lee, Spike with Ralph Wiley. By Any Means Necessary: The Trials and Tribulations of The Making Of Malcolm X. New York, N.Y.: Hyperion, 1992.

* Lincoln, C. Eric. The Black Muslims in America. Boston, Beacon. 1961.

* Lomax, Louis. To Kill a Black Man. Los Angeles: Holloway House, 1968.

* Lomax, Louis. When the Word is Given. Cleveland: World Publishing, 1963.

* Maglangbayan, Shawna. Garvey, Lumumba, and Malcolm: National-Separatists. Chicago, Third World Press 1972.

* Marable, Manning. On Malcolm X: His Message & Meaning. Westfield, N.J.: Open Media, 1992.

* Martin, Tony. Race First. Westport, Connecticut: Greenwood, 1976.

* Myers, Walter Dean. Malcolm X By Any Means Necessary. New York: Scholastic, 1993.

* Natambu, Kofi. The Life and Work of Malcolm X. Indianapolis: Alpha Books, 2002.

* Perry, Bruce. Malcolm: The Life of A Man Who Changed Black America. New York: Station Hill, 1991.

* Randall, Dudley and Margaret G. Burroughs, ed. For Malcolm; Poems on The Life and The Death of Malcolm X. Preface and Eulogy By Ossie Davis. Detroit: Broadside Press, 1967.

* Rickford, Russell J. Betty Shabazz: A Remarkable Story of Survival and Faith Before and After Malcolm X. Naperville, IL: Sourcebooks, 2003.

* Sales, William W. From Civil Rights To Black Liberation: Malcolm X And The Organization Of Afro-American Unity. Boston, MA: South End Press, 1994.

* Shabazz, Ilyasah. Growing Up X. New York: One World, 2002.

* Strickland, William, et al. Malcolm X: Make It Plain. Penguin Books, 1994.

* Terrill, Robert. Malcolm X: Inventing Radical Judgment. Michigan State University Press, 2004.

* T'Shaka, Oba. The Political Legacy of Malcolm X. Richmond, Calif.: Pan Afrikan Publications, 1983.

* Tuttle, William. Race Riot: Chicago, The Red Summer of 1919. New York: Atheneum, 1970.

* Vincent, Theodore. Black Power and the Garvey Movement. San Francisco: Ramparts, 1972.

* Wolfenstein, Eugene Victor. The Victims of Democracy: Malcolm X and the Black Revolution. London: Free Association Books, 1989.

* Wood, Joe, ed. Malcolm X: In Our Own Image. New York: St. Martin's Press, 1992.

* Woodward, C. Vann. Origins of the New South. Baton Rouge: Louisiana State University Press, 1967.

GNU Free Documentation License

Version 1.2, November 2002

0. PREAMBLE

The purpose of this License is to make a manual, textbook, or other functional and useful document "free" in the sense of freedom: to assure everyone the effective freedom to copy and redistribute it, with or without modifying it, either commercially or noncommercially. Secondarily, this License preserves for the author and publisher a way to get credit for their work, while not being considered responsible for modifications made by others.

This License is a kind of "copyleft", which means that derivative works of the document must themselves be free in the same sense. It complements the GNU General Public License, which is a copyleft license designed for free software.

We have designed this License in order to use it for manuals for free software, because free software needs free documentation: a free program should come with manuals providing the same freedoms that the software does. But this License is not limited to software manuals; it can be used for any textual work, regardless of subject matter or whether it is published as a printed book. We recommend this License principally for works whose purpose is instruction or reference.

Black Muslim Leader

1. APPLICABILITY AND DEFINITIONS

This License applies to any manual or other work, in any medium, that contains a notice placed by the copyright holder saying it can be distributed under the terms of this License. Such a notice grants a world-wide, royalty-free license, unlimited in duration, to use that work under the conditions stated herein. The "Document", below, refers to any such manual or work. Any member of the public is a licensee, and is addressed as "you". You accept the license if you copy, modify or distribute the work in a way requiring permission under copyright law.

A "Modified Version" of the Document means any work containing the Document or a portion of it, either copied verbatim, or with modifications and/or translated into another language.

A "Secondary Section" is a named appendix or a front-matter section of the Document that deals exclusively with the relationship of the publishers or authors of the Document to the Document's overall subject (or to related matters) and contains nothing that could fall directly within that overall subject. (Thus, if the Document is in part a textbook of mathematics, a Secondary Section may not explain any mathematics.) The relationship could be a matter of historical connection with the subject or with related matters, or of legal, commercial, philosophical, ethical or political position regarding them.

The "Invariant Sections" are certain Secondary Sections whose titles are designated, as being those of Invariant Sections, in the notice that says that the Document is released under this License. If a section does not fit the above definition of Secondary then it is not allowed to be designated as Invariant. The Document may contain zero Invariant Sections. If the Document does not identify any Invariant Sections then there are none.

The "Cover Texts" are certain short passages of text that are listed, as Front-Cover Texts or Back-Cover Texts, in the notice that says that the Document is released under this License. A Front-Cover Text may be at most 5 words, and a Back-Cover Text may be at most 25 words.

A "Transparent" copy of the Document means a machine-readable copy, represented in a format whose specification is available to the general public, that is suitable for revising the document straightforwardly with generic text editors or (for images composed of pixels) generic paint programs or (for drawings) some widely available drawing editor, and that is suitable for input to text formatters or for automatic translation to a variety of formats suitable for input to text formatters. A copy made in an otherwise Transparent file format whose markup, or absence of markup, has been arranged to thwart or discourage subsequent modification by readers is not Transparent. An image format is not Transparent if used for any substantial amount of text. A copy that is not "Transparent" is called "Opaque".

Examples of suitable formats for Transparent copies include plain ASCII without markup, Texinfo input format, LaTeX input format, SGML or XML using a publicly available DTD, and standard-conforming simple HTML, PostScript or PDF designed for human modification. Examples of transparent image formats include PNG, XCF and JPG. Opaque formats include proprietary formats that can be read and edited only by proprietary word processors, SGML or XML for which the DTD and/or processing tools are not generally available, and the machine-generated HTML, PostScript or PDF produced by some word processors for output purposes only.

The "Title Page" means, for a printed book, the title page itself, plus such following pages as are needed to hold, legibly, the material this License requires to appear in the title page. For works in formats which do not have any title page as such, "Title Page" means the text near the most prominent appearance of the work's title, preceding the beginning of the body of the text.

A section "Entitled XYZ" means a named subunit of the Document whose title either is precisely XYZ or contains XYZ in parentheses following text that translates XYZ in another language. (Here XYZ stands for a specific section name mentioned below, such as "Acknowledgements", "Dedications", "Endorsements", or "History".) To "Preserve the Title" of such a section when you modify the Document means that it remains a section "Entitled XYZ" according to this definition.

The Document may include Warranty Disclaimers next to the notice which states that this License applies to the Document. These Warranty Disclaimers are considered to be included by reference in this License, but only as regards disclaiming warranties: any other implication that these Warranty Disclaimers may have is void and has no effect on the meaning of this License.

2. VERBATIM COPYING

You may copy and distribute the Document in any medium, either commercially or noncommercially, provided that this License, the copyright notices, and the license notice saying this License applies to the Document are reproduced in all copies, and that you add no other conditions whatsoever to those of this License. You may not use technical measures to obstruct or control the reading or further copying of the copies you make or distribute. However, you may accept compensation in exchange for copies. If you distribute a large enough number of copies you must also follow the conditions in section 3.

You may also lend copies, under the same conditions stated above, and you may publicly display copies.

3. COPYING IN QUANTITY

If you publish printed copies (or copies in media that commonly have printed covers) of the Document, numbering more than 100, and the Document's license notice requires Cover Texts, you must enclose the copies in covers that carry, clearly and legibly, all these Cover Texts: Front-Cover Texts on the front cover, and Back-Cover Texts on the back cover. Both covers must also clearly and legibly identify you as the publisher of these copies. The front cover must present the full title with all words of the title equally prominent and visible. You may add other material on the covers in addition. Copying with changes limited to the covers, as long as they preserve the title of the Document and satisfy these conditions, can be treated as verbatim copying in other respects.

If the required texts for either cover are too voluminous to fit legibly, you should put the first ones listed (as many as fit reasonably) on the actual cover, and continue the rest onto adjacent pages.

If you publish or distribute Opaque copies of the Document numbering more than 100, you must either include a machine-readable Transparent copy along with each Opaque copy, or state in or with each Opaque copy a computer-network location from which the general network-using public has access to download using public-standard network protocols a complete Transparent copy of the Document, free of added material. If you use the latter option, you must take reasonably prudent steps, when you begin distribution of Opaque copies in quantity, to ensure that this Transparent copy will remain thus accessible at the stated location until at least one year after the last time you distribute an Opaque copy (directly or through your agents or retailers) of that edition to the public.

It is requested, but not required, that you contact the authors of the Document well before redistributing any large number of copies, to give them a chance to provide you with an updated version of the Document.

4. MODIFICATIONS

You may copy and distribute a Modified Version of the Document under the conditions of sections 2 and 3 above, provided that you release the Modified Version under precisely this License, with the Modified Version filling the role of the Document, thus licensing distribution and modification of the Modified Version to whoever possesses a copy of it. In addition, you must do these things in the Modified Version:

* A. Use in the Title Page (and on the covers, if any) a title distinct from that of the Document, and from those of previous versions (which should, if there were any, be listed in the History section of the Document). You may use the same title as a previous version if the original publisher of that version gives permission.
* B. List on the Title Page, as authors, one or more persons or entities responsible for authorship of the modifications in the Modified Version, together with at least five of the principal authors of the Document (all of its principal authors, if it has fewer than five), unless they release you from this requirement.
* C. State on the Title page the name of the publisher of the Modified Version, as the publisher.
* D. Preserve all the copyright notices of the Document.

* E. Add an appropriate copyright notice for your modifications adjacent to the other copyright notices.

* F. Include, immediately after the copyright notices, a license notice giving the public permission to use the Modified Version under the terms of this License, in the form shown in the Addendum below.

* G. Preserve in that license notice the full lists of Invariant Sections and required Cover Texts given in the Document's license notice.

* H. Include an unaltered copy of this License.

* I. Preserve the section Entitled "History", Preserve its Title, and add to it an item stating at least the title, year, new authors, and publisher of the Modified Version as given on the Title Page. If there is no section Entitled "History" in the Document, create one stating the title, year, authors, and publisher of the Document as given on its Title Page, then add an item describing the Modified Version as stated in the previous sentence.

* J. Preserve the network location, if any, given in the Document for public access to a Transparent copy of the Document, and likewise the network locations given in the Document for previous versions it was based on. These may be placed in the "History" section. You may omit a network location for a work that was published at least four years before the Document itself, or if the original publisher of the version it refers to gives permission.

* K. For any section Entitled "Acknowledgements" or "Dedications", Preserve the Title of the section, and preserve in the section all the substance and tone of each of the contributor acknowledgements and/or dedications given therein.

* L. Preserve all the Invariant Sections of the Document, unaltered in their text and in their titles. Section numbers or the equivalent are not considered part of the section titles.

* M. Delete any section Entitled "Endorsements". Such a section may not be included in the Modified Version.

* N. Do not retitle any existing section to be Entitled "Endorsements" or to conflict in title with any Invariant Section.

* O. Preserve any Warranty Disclaimers.

If the Modified Version includes new front-matter sections or appendices that qualify as Secondary Sections and contain no material copied from the Document, you may at your option designate some or all of these sections as invariant. To do this, add their titles to the list of Invariant Sections in the

Modified Version's license notice. These titles must be distinct from any other section titles.

You may add a section Entitled "Endorsements", provided it contains nothing but endorsements of your Modified Version by various parties--for example, statements of peer review or that the text has been approved by an organization as the authoritative definition of a standard.

You may add a passage of up to five words as a Front-Cover Text, and a passage of up to 25 words as a Back-Cover Text, to the end of the list of Cover Texts in the Modified Version. Only one passage of Front-Cover Text and one of Back-Cover Text may be added by (or through arrangements made by) any one entity. If the Document already includes a cover text for the same cover, previously added by you or by arrangement made by the same entity you are acting on behalf of, you may not add another; but you may replace the old one, on explicit permission from the previous publisher that added the old one.

The author(s) and publisher(s) of the Document do not by this License give permission to use their names for publicity for or to assert or imply endorsement of any Modified Version.

5. COMBINING DOCUMENTS

You may combine the Document with other documents released under this License, under the terms defined in section 4 above for modified versions, provided that you include in the combination all of the Invariant Sections of all of the original documents, unmodified, and list them all as Invariant Sections of your combined work in its license notice, and that you preserve all their Warranty Disclaimers.

The combined work need only contain one copy of this License, and multiple identical Invariant Sections may be replaced with a single copy. If there are multiple Invariant Sections with the same name but different contents, make the title of each such section unique by adding at the end of it, in parentheses, the name of the original author or publisher of that section if known, or else a unique number. Make the same adjustment to the section titles in the list of Invariant Sections in the license notice of the combined work.

In the combination, you must combine any sections Entitled "History" in the various original documents, forming one section Entitled "History"; likewise combine any sections Entitled "Acknowledgements", and any sections Entitled "Dedications". You must delete all sections Entitled "Endorsements."

6. COLLECTIONS OF DOCUMENTS

You may make a collection consisting of the Document and other documents released under this License, and replace the individual copies of this License in the various documents with a single copy that is included in the collection, provided that you follow the rules of this License for verbatim copying of each of the documents in all other respects.

You may extract a single document from such a collection, and distribute it individually under this License, provided you insert a copy of this License into the extracted document, and follow this License in all other respects regarding verbatim copying of that document.

7. AGGREGATION WITH INDEPENDENT WORKS

A compilation of the Document or its derivatives with other separate and independent documents or works, in or on a volume of a storage or distribution medium, is called an "aggregate" if the copyright resulting from the compilation is not used to limit the legal rights of the compilation's users beyond what the individual works permit. When the Document is included in an aggregate, this License does not apply to the other works in the aggregate which are not themselves derivative works of the Document.

If the Cover Text requirement of section 3 is applicable to these copies of the Document, then if the Document is less than one half of the entire aggregate, the Document's Cover Texts may be placed on covers that bracket the Document within the aggregate, or the electronic equivalent of covers if the Document is in electronic form. Otherwise they must appear on printed covers that bracket the whole aggregate.

8. TRANSLATION

Translation is considered a kind of modification, so you may distribute translations of the Document under the terms of section 4. Replacing Invariant Sections with translations requires special permission from their copyright holders, but you may include translations of some or all Invariant Sections in addition to the original versions of these Invariant Sections. You may include a translation of this License, and all the license notices in the Document, and any Warranty Disclaimers, provided that you also include the original English version of this License and the original versions of those notices and disclaimers. In case of a disagreement between the translation and the original version of this License or a notice or disclaimer, the original version will prevail.

If a section in the Document is Entitled "Acknowledgements", "Dedications", or "History", the requirement (section 4) to Preserve its Title (section 1) will typically require changing the actual title.

9. TERMINATION

You may not copy, modify, sublicense, or distribute the Document except as expressly provided for under this License. Any other attempt to copy, modify, sublicense or distribute the Document is void, and will automatically terminate your rights under this License. However, parties who have received copies, or rights, from you under this License will not have their licenses terminated so long as such parties remain in full compliance.

10. FUTURE REVISIONS OF THIS LICENSE

The Free Software Foundation may publish new, revised versions of the GNU Free Documentation License from time to time. Such new versions will be similar in spirit to the present version, but may differ in detail to address new problems or concerns. See http://www.gnu.org/copyleft/.

Each version of the License is given a distinguishing version number. If the Document specifies that a particular numbered version of this License "or any later version" applies to it, you have the option of following the terms and conditions either of that specified version or of any later version that has been published (not as a draft) by the Free Software Foundation. If the Document does not specify a version number of this License, you may choose any version ever published (not as a draft) by the Free Software Foundation.

How to use this License for your documents

To use this License in a document you have written, include a copy of the License in the document and put the following copyright and license notices just after the title page:

Copyright (c) YEAR YOUR NAME.
Permission is granted to copy, distribute and/or modify this document under the terms of the GNU Free Documentation License, Version 1.2 or any later version published by the Free Software Foundation; with no Invariant Sections, no Front-Cover Texts, and no Back-Cover Texts. A copy of the license is included in the section entitled "GNU
Free Documentation License".

If you have Invariant Sections, Front-Cover Texts and Back-Cover Texts, replace the "with...Texts." line with this:

with the Invariant Sections being LIST THEIR TITLES, with the Front-Cover Texts being LIST, and with the Back-Cover Texts being LIST.

If you have Invariant Sections without Cover Texts, or some other combination of the three, merge those two alternatives to suit the situation.

If your document contains nontrivial examples of program code, we recommend releasing these examples in parallel under your choice of free software license, such as the GNU General Public License, to permit their use in free software.

Printed in the United States
128736LV00008B/12/P

9 781599 861326